D1119963

First Facts™

From Farm to Table

From Tomato to Ketchup

by Roberta Basel

Consultant:
Art Hill, Professor of Food Science
University of Guelph
Guelph, Ontario, Canada

Capstone
press

Mankato, Minnesota

First Facts is published by Capstone Press,
151 Good Counsel Drive, P.O. Box 669, Mankato, Minnesota 56002.
www.capstonepress.com

Library of Congress Cataloging-in-Publication Data
Basel, Roberta.
From tomato to ketchup / by Roberta Basel.
    p. cm.—(First facts. From farm to table)
    Includes bibliographical references (p. 23) and index.
    ISBN 0-7368-4286-1 (hardcover)
    1. Ketchup—Juvenile literature. 2. Tomatoes—Juvenile literature. I. Title. II. Series.
TX819.K48B37 2006
641.8'14—dc22   2004029484

Summary: An introduction to the basic concept of food production, distribution, and consumption
    by tracing the production of ketchup from tomatoes to the finished product.

Editorial Credits
Jennifer Besel, editor; Jennifer Bergstrom, set designer; Ted Williams, book designer;
    Wanda Winch, photo researcher/photo editor

Photo Credits
Bruce Coleman Inc./John Elk III, 6–7
Capstone Press/Karon Dubke, cover, 1, 5, 19, 21
Comstock, back cover
David R. Frazier Photolibrary, 9
Grant Heilman Photography/Alan Pitcairn, 8; Larry Lefever, 10, 12–13
The Image Finders/Mark E. Gibson, 11
Mike Gassman, 20
Photo courtesy of Red Gold LLC, 14, 17

Table of Contents

Fun for Food

Ketchup adds color and flavor to food. Many people eat ketchup on hot dogs, hamburgers, and french fries. Some people even put it on eggs and spaghetti.

Ketchup has to be made before people can eat it. Making ketchup takes many steps.

Fun Fact!
Ketchup is also called catchup and catsup.

Tomatoes

Ketchup is made from tomatoes. Tomatoes are grown in fields. Farmers put seeds in the ground. Tomato plants grow from these seeds.

Tomatoes grow in many shapes and sizes. Different kinds of tomatoes are used to make ketchup.

Fun Fact!
The largest tomato ever grown weighed 7 pounds (3 kilograms).

Picking Tomatoes

Farmers use a **machine** to pick tomatoes.
The machine scoops up whole tomato plants.
It shakes the tomatoes off the plants.

The machine puts good tomatoes
into trailers. It drops bad tomatoes
on the ground.

To the Factory

Trucks pull the trailers of tomatoes to the **grading station**. There, people check the tomatoes. The good tomatoes are taken to the ketchup **factory**.

Workers use water to unload the tomatoes. The tomatoes float on water into the ketchup factory.

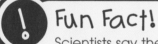

Fun Fact!

Scientists say the tomato is a fruit. But in 1893, the U.S. Supreme Court ruled the tomato should be called a vegetable.

Making Ketchup

At the factory, the tomatoes are chopped and put into large pots. As the tomatoes cook, machines and people add **ingredients**. These ingredients often include sugar, salt, and spices.

Fun Fact!
Each American eats about 22 pounds (10 kilograms) of tomatoes every year.

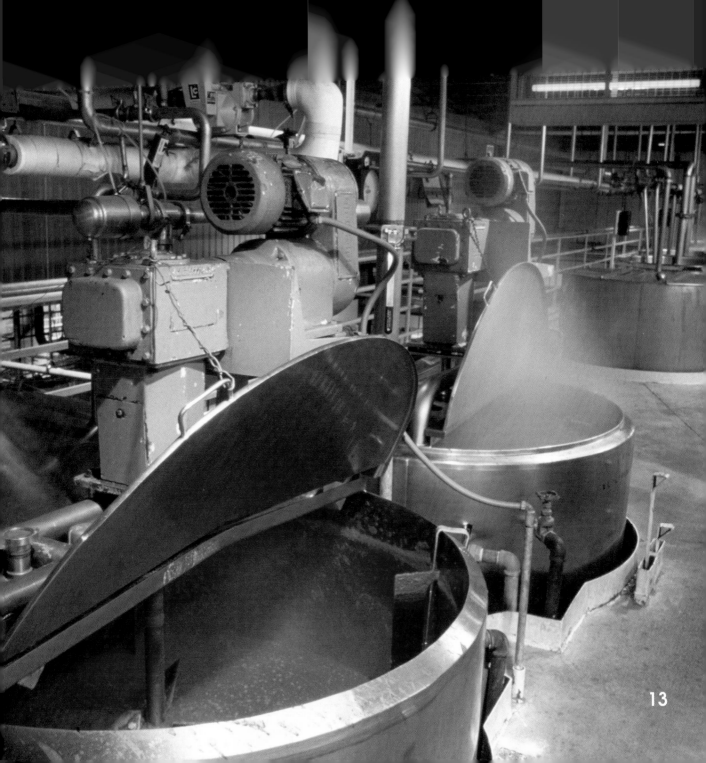

Finishing

After the ketchup is cooked, it is put through screens called finishers. The screens catch the seeds and skins.

The liquid part goes through the screens and into another machine. This machine takes the air out of the ketchup. Ketchup lasts longer without air in it.

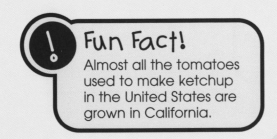

Fun Fact!
Almost all the tomatoes used to make ketchup in the United States are grown in California.

To the Store

Machines squirt the ketchup into glass or plastic bottles. Other machines put caps and labels on the bottles.

The bottles are put in large boxes. Workers load the boxes in trucks and trains. The trucks and trains carry the ketchup to stores.

! Fun Fact!
Ketchup can be found in 97 percent of all American homes.

Where to Find Ketchup

People can find ketchup in many places. Ketchup is sold in every grocery store. Some stores sell different kinds of ketchup. It can be plain or spicy. Ketchup can add flavor to any meal.

Fun Fact!
Each American uses about three bottles of ketchup every year.

Amazing but True!

The world's largest ketchup bottle is in Collinsville, Illinois. It stands 170 feet (52 meters) high. This ketchup bottle is actually a water tower. It was built in 1949. People can still visit the ketchup bottle today.

Hands On: Homemade Ketchup

Make your own ketchup. Ask an adult to help you.

What You Need

measuring cups and spoons
6 oz. (170 grams) tomato paste
½ cup (120 mL) light corn syrup
½ cup (120 mL) white vinegar
¼ cup (60 mL) water
1 tbsp. (15 mL) sugar

1 tsp. (5 mL) salt
¼ tsp. (1.2 mL) onion powder
⅛ tsp. (.6 mL) garlic powder
medium-sized saucepan
mixing spoon

What You Do

1. Put all of the ingredients into the saucepan.
2. Stir the ingredients as you cook the mixture over medium heat. The mixture should become smooth. Heat the mixture until it boils.
3. Turn the heat to low. Let the mixture cook for 20 minutes. Stir it often as it cooks.
4. Take the saucepan off the stove. Cover the saucepan. Let the mixture cool. Your ketchup is done.
5. Keep your ketchup in a sealed container in the refrigerator.

Makes 1½ cups (360 mL)

Glossary

factory (FAK-tuh-ree)—a building where products are made in large numbers; factories often use machines to make products.

grading station (GRAYD-ing STAY-shuhn)—a place where good and bad tomatoes are sorted

ingredient (in-GREE-dee-uhnt)—an item used to make something else

machine (muh-SHEEN)—a piece of equipment that is used to do a job

Read More

Franck, Irene M., and David Brownstone. *Tomatoes.* Riches of the Earth. Danbury, Conn.: Grolier, 2003.

Snyder, Inez. *Tomatoes.* Harvesttime. New York: Children's Press, 2004.

Internet Sites

FactHound offers a safe, fun way to find Internet sites related to this book. All of the sites on FactHound have been researched by our staff.

Here's how:
1. Visit *www.facthound.com*
2. Type in this special code **0736842861** for age-appropriate sites. Or enter a search word related to this book for a more general search.
3. Click on the **Fetch It** button.

FactHound will fetch the best sites for you!

Index